Parent's Introduction

Whether your child is a beginning reader, a reluctant reader, or an eager reader, this book offers a fun and easy way to encourage and help your child in reading.

Developed with reading education specialists, **We Both Read** books invite you and your child to take turns reading aloud. You read the left-hand pages of the book, and your child reads the right-hand pages—which have been written at one of six early reading levels. The result is a wonderful new reading experience and faster reading development!

You may find it helpful to read the entire book aloud yourself the first time, then invite your child to participate the second time. As you read, try to make the story come alive by reading with expression. This will help to model good fluency.

In some books, a few challenging words are introduced in the parent's text with **bold** lettering. Pointing out and discussing these words can help to build your child's reading vocabulary. If your child is a beginning reader, it may be helpful to run a finger under the text as each of you reads. To help show whose turn it is, a blue dot ● comes before text for you to read, and a red star ★ comes before text for your child to read.

If your child struggles with a word, you can encourage "sounding it out," but keep in mind that this will not help with all words because some words don't follow phonetic patterns.

You can help with breaking down the sounds of the letters or syllables, but if your child becomes too frustrated, it is usually best to simply say the word.

While reading together, try to help your child understand what is being read. It can help to stop every few pages to ask questions about the text and check if there are any words your child doesn't understand. After you finish the book, ask a few more questions or discuss what you've read together. Rereading this book multiple times may also help your child to read with more ease and understanding.

Most importantly, remember to praise your child's efforts and keep the reading fun. Keep the tips above in mind, but don't worry about doing everything right. Simply sharing the enjoyment of reading together will increase your child's reading skills and help to start your child on a lifetime of reading enjoyment!

Trucks

A We Both Read® Book: Level K–1
Guided Reading: Level C

Text Copyright © 2024 by Sindy McKay
Use of photographs provided by iStock and Dreamstime
All rights reserved

We Both Read® is a trademark of Treasure Bay, Inc.

Published by
Treasure Bay, Inc.
PO Box 519
Roseville, CA 95661 USA

Printed in China

Library of Congress Control Number: 2023905583

ISBN: 978-1-60115-375-3

Visit us online at:
WeBothRead.com

PR-10-23

TRUCKS

By Sindy McKay

TREASURE BAY

- Honk! Honk! It seems like everywhere you go there are trucks on the road!

You see pick-up trucks, delivery trucks…

★ ...and big rigs!

- Trucks are large vehicles that can carry things from one place to another.

Maybe you have spotted one that is carrying food. At a special loading dock, food is put…

★ …in the truck.

- The truck then drives to the **store** where it may back into a receiving dock. Here the food is unloaded and goes into…

★ ...the **store**.

- They can carry logs, or space shuttles, . . .

★ . . . or cars.

- A truck can help you **move** to a new **house**.

★ Or **move** the **house** to you!

- Tanker trucks **haul** liquids in big tanks. The tanks may contain water, milk, or gas.

★ Dump trucks can **haul** rocks.

- Most mail is delivered in a mail truck. A mail person makes deliveries in all kinds of weather, even in . . .

★ …the snow.

- These trucks deliver purchased items directly to your home. Some of the items are made in far off lands then shipped across the ocean in containers…

★ …on big ships.

- When the ships arrive at the port, the containers are put onto large container trucks to be taken to warehouses.

From the warehouses, these items are carried by truck to various stores. Now they are ready…

★ …to sell!

- Many trucks bring things to you. Some, like garbage and recycling trucks, take things away.

This truck takes crushed aluminum cans away to the recycling center.

★ This truck picks up trash bins.

- **Your** garbage isn't the only thing trucks remove. They can remove snow.

They can remove dead branches. And, if you park in the wrong place, they can remove . . .

★ ...**your** car!

- Certain trucks help keep us safe. Hook and ladder **fire** trucks are used to rescue people from tall buildings and other high places. Other **fire** trucks carry hoses that are used to help…

★ ...stop a **fire**.

- An armored truck is used to safely transport money. It is like a giant metal safe.

An ambulance, or emergency services truck, takes people to get medical care.

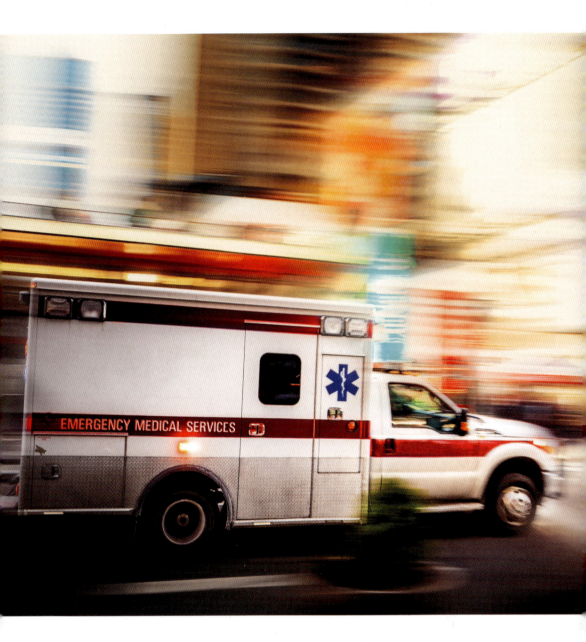

★ It can go fast!

- Workers use boom bucket trucks to reach **high** places to do repairs, wash windows, trim trees, and many other important jobs.

★ That is **high!**

- Some trucks can lift their containers high in the air to load supplies onto jet planes.

Some have a long, low **flatbed**. Very large items can be carried…

★ …on a **flatbed!**

- Trucks are especially useful on a farm. This hay baler rolls the hay into cylinders which are then loaded onto a flatbed behind a pick-up truck.

★ It takes the hay away.

- Food trucks can be found just about anywhere that people get hungry.

Taco trucks are especially popular!

★ This truck sells ice cream.

- **Monster** trucks are specially made pickups with **cool**-looking oversized tires that allow them to race over rough terrain. They often do amazing stunts where they drive over old cars, crushing them.

★ **Monster** trucks are **cool**!

- There are many types of trucks and many ways to use them. The next time you are on the road, see how many different kinds you can see.

★ Honk! Honk!

Glossary

big rig
a truck, sometimes called a semi or a tractor-trailer, which has 18 wheels and a large trailer used to transport many types of freight

tanker
a vehicle with a large tank used to transport liquids, such as milk or gas

armored truck
a vehicle used to transport cash or other valuable items

boom bucket
a bucket-shaped device attached to a truck with a long extension arm that is used to reach high places

flatbed
a truck with a low, flat area for carrying large, long items

monster truck
a specialized off-road performance vehicle with four-wheel steering, a large engine, and huge tires

Questions to Ask after Reading

Add to the benefits of reading this book by discussing answers to these questions. Also consider discussing a few of your own questions.

1. What are some differences between trucks and cars?

2. Name as many things as you can that a truck might carry.

3. If you were to drive a truck, what kind of truck would you most like to drive? Why?

4. What kinds of equipment might you find on a fire truck?

If you liked *Trucks,* here are some other
We Both Read® books you are sure to enjoy!

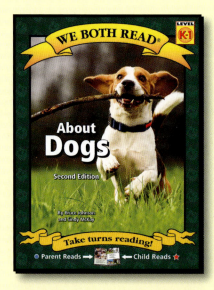
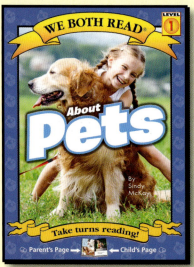
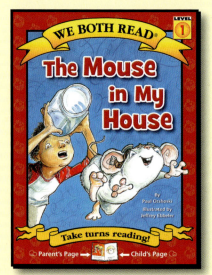

To see all the We Both Read books that are available,
just go online to **WeBothRead.com**.